Alexander Hamilton

A SHORT BIOGRAPHY

By Doug West, Ph.D.

Alexander Hamilton – A Short Biography

Copyright © 2016 Doug West

Table of Contents

Preface

Welcome to the book *Alexander Hamilton – A Short Biography*. This book is part of the 30 Minute Book Series and, as the name of the series implies, if you are an average reader this book will take around 30 minutes to read or a little longer to listen to in audio format. Since this book is not meant to be an all-encompassing biography of Alexander Hamilton, you may want to know more about this great man and his accomplishments. To help you with this, there are several good references at the end of this book. Thank you for purchasing this book and I hope you enjoy your time reading about Alexander Hamilton.

Doug West

January 2016

Introduction

Alexander Hamilton, born in the British West Indies, was an outsider from the very beginning. His illegitimate birth drove him to prove his worthiness to others throughout his life. His quest for honor was one of the defining characteristics that colored his decisions. Hamilton was a small man with a large ambition, and this would drive him to greatness and create some powerful enemies in his wake.

Alexander Hamilton's life was not without its share of tragedy. Before his fifteenth birthday, his father had abandoned the family and his mother had died of yellow fever. Luckily for young Alexander, a group of benefactors realized his potential and paid to have him sent to the British colony, America, for an education.

While attending King's College in New York, Hamilton caught the revolutionary spirit and volunteered in the Continental Army to fight against the British. He soon distinguished himself and would serve as General George Washington's aide-de-camp during much of the Revolutionary War.

After the Revolutionary War, Hamilton returned to his law practice and soon entered politics. In 1787, he would help draft the Constitution of the United States and then write a series of critical essays, called the *Federalist Papers*, which were key to ratification of the Constitution. Hamilton's position on the role of government was for a strong Federal government.

President Washington nominated Hamilton to become the first Secretary of the Treasury — which was quickly approved by the Senate. During his tenure as Secretary of the Treasury, he set the nation on a sound fiscal footing, established the first national bank and a mint to produce coinage. Hamilton was a master of setting up institutions within the government and making bitter enemies of powerful men, such as John Adams, Thomas Jefferson, and Aaron Burr.

One of Hamilton's political rivalries would turn very personal as Aaron Burr, the sitting Vice President of the United States, was seeking retaliation for Hamilton's disparaging remarks. Hamilton's honor would not let him decline Burr's challenge to a duel. The outcome of the duel was fatal for Alexander Hamilton — dead at age forty-nine, leaving behind a wife, seven living children, and a legacy that would survive the centuries.

Read on and see this life of triumph and tragedy unfold.

CHAPTER 1

Early Years

Opinion, whether well or ill founded, is the governing principle of human affairs. – Alexander Hamilton

Unlike some of the other founding fathers, such as George Washington or John Hancock, Alexander Hamilton was not born into a well-to-do family with plenty of money and prominence. Alexander was born on January 11, 1755, on the small island of Nevis in the British West Indies. The island measures nine miles in its longest dimensions and, like many of the islands at that point in history and in that part of the Caribbean Sea, the main business was sugar cane plantations manned with slave labor from Africa. New slaves were imported yearly to most plantations as the life expectancy of the slaves was only a few years due to the hard labor, excessive heat, and regular outbreaks of yellow fever.

Alexander's mother was Rachel Fawcett, who was originally married to a Danish Jew named John Michael Levine. Levine owned a small plantation on St. Croix Island and abandoned Rachel after five years of marriage. After the marriage dissolved, Rachel took up with a Scotsman named James Hamilton, with whom she had two sons. Her divorce decree with

Levine did not allow her to re-marry, which resulted in both the Hamilton boys being illegitimate in the eyes of the Danish authorities. The illegitimate nature of Alexander Hamilton's birth would be a recurring sore spot for the remainder of his life.

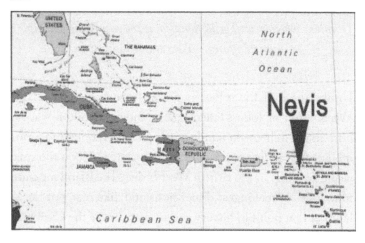

Figure – Map of West Indies

The young Hamilton boys would meet with a succession of personal disasters over the next few years. Their father, James Hamilton, was rather lazy and a poor businessman, and within a few years he had left the family in financial ruin. Like Rachel's first husband, James abandoned the family. Another disastrous life event occurred when Rachel died of yellow fever when Alexander was only 13 years old. Due to the illegitimate nature of the boy's birth, he was left with virtually nothing of his mother's estate. The only physical possessions left to him were a few books.

Alexander helped supported himself by working at a counting house on St. Croix Island owned by Nicholas Cruger. The owner of the business fell ill and young Hamilton ran the business for six months while Mr. Cruger recovered. Alexander's skills and knowledge beyond his years became evident to those who knew him on the island. With the help of some of the local men, Hamilton was given the opportunity to sail for America in 1773 to attend school. He first spent a year in New Jersey at a grammar school, then attended King's College in New York City. King's College would become Columbia University.

CHAPTER 2

Making of a Revolutionary

The passions of a revolution are apt to hurry even good men into excess. – Alexander Hamilton

While in college, Hamilton's political savvy became apparent as he began to submit articles to Holt's *New York Journal*, or *General Advertiser*. He thought of himself as a writer and by his twentieth birthday he had published two pamphlets which helped launch his political career. The two pamphlets written by Hamilton were published anonymously, which was the custom of the time. The first work was entitled *A Full Vindication of the Measures of the Congress* and the second was *The Farmer Refuted.* The two pamphlets appeared in the years 1774 to 1775, which were critical years just before the start of the Revolutionary War. Hamilton's work took the position of a defense of American colonists' position against England. His pamphlets revealed a deep insight into the problems between the colonists and the British crown and they were well received by his contemporaries.

Hamilton was small in stature, slender with reddish hair, and possessed a burning ambition. The hardships of his youth had taught young Hamilton to be a hard-headed realist, unburdened by idealism or sentimentality. His quick wit and driving ambition caused him to appear arrogant and tactless to those around him. This lack of social polish in his later life would result in the creation of powerful enemies.

King's College was a small college with only twenty-four undergraduates and six medical students. The president of the school was Myles Cooper, an Oxford University educated British loyalist who had taken Anglican orders. The school was associated with the Church of England and morning and evening prayer services were to be attended by the students. Though the school was small, it had a large library with over fifteen hundred books supplied by English benefactors. Hamilton was a voracious reader and took advantage of the library.

Hamilton was leading a dual life during his time in college; during the day he was a dutiful student at a college run by British loyalists, and at night he would consort with rebels interested in independence for America. In May of 1775, Hamilton's allegiance to the college and its President, Reverend Cooper, was to be tested. An angry mob of rebels approached the college looking to do harm to Myles Cooper. Hamilton took immediate action and positioned himself on the stoop of the college and proceeded to argue with the crowd that they were wrong and this was not what the cause of liberty was about. Hamilton was successful in slowing the crowd long enough for Cooper to escape over the back fence, after which he ended up staying with a fellow loyalist until he could sail for England.

Figure – Captain Alexander Hamilton

At the outbreak of the war for independence with Britain, he organized an artillery company and became its captain. A fellow officer recalled his first sight of Hamilton: "I noticed a youth, a mere stripling, small, slender, almost delicate in frame, marching beside a piece of artillery with a cocked hat pulled down over his eyes, apparently lost in thought, with his hand resting on the cannon and every now and then patting it as he mused, as if it were a favorite horse or a pet plaything."

Hamilton's initiative didn't go unnoticed as he caught the attention of General Nathanael Greene, who introduced Hamilton to the leader of the Continental Army, General George Washington. Washington was also impressed with Hamilton and in March 1777 he appointed him as his aide-de-camp with the rank of lieutenant colonel. Hamilton's skill as a writer was invaluable to Washington as he would prepare much of Washington's correspondence for the General's signature.

During the winter of 1777, Hamilton met his future wife. While on an intelligence gathering mission for General Washington, he stayed for four days at the home of General Phillip Schuyler in Albany, New York. It was there that Hamilton met Schuyler's five daughters, one of whom was named Elizabeth.

Armies in the eighteenth century seldom fought during the winter months and this was a time for parties and rest and, in Alexander Hamilton's case, romance. Hamilton and Elizabeth "Betsy" Schuyler would meet again in February 1780 in Morristown, New Jersey, and Hamilton was apparently swept off his feet. He wrote to a friend of Betsy: "Most unmercifully handsome and so perverse that she has none of those pretty affectations, which are the prerogatives of beauty…She has good nature, affability and vivacity unembellished with that charm frivolousness which is justly deemed one of the principal accomplishments of a belle." After a courtship of several months, the couple was wed on December 14, 1780, at Schuyler's mansion in Albany, New York. Their long marriage, though not without troubles, would result in eight children.

Figure – Elizabeth Schuyler

After four years as Washington's aide, Hamilton sought a more active role in the military as a leader of men in battle. After a falling out with Washington, the General granted his wish and gave him a field officer position. Hamilton did lead a successful storming party of American and French soldiers at the battle of Yorktown, Virginia in 1781. This was the last major battle in the war and the English commander Lord Cornwallis would surrender within days.

CHAPTER 3

Legal Practice and the Constitution

I have thought it my duty to exhibit things as they are, not as they ought to be. – Alexander Hamilton

In July of 1782, Hamilton was appointed to the Congress of the Confederation as a New York representative. One of the on-going hot issues discussed in Congress was the authority of the central government to raise revenue through taxation. The lack of stable sources of funds for the new government was a weakness of the Articles of Confederation. Hamilton had been frustrated by the shortcomings of the central government and drafted a call to revise the Articles of Confederation. The resolution contains many features of the future United States Constitution, including a strong federal government with the ability to collect taxes, raise an army, and provide for the separation of powers into the Executive, Legislative, and Judicial branches.

After Hamilton resigned from Congress, he began to study the law to become a lawyer. After several months of self-directed study, he was authorized to practice law in New York. Hamilton and his partner, Richard Harrison, specialized in defending Tories and British subjects. He became one of New York City's most successful lawyers. Hamilton could not resist becoming involved in politics again as he was dismayed at the lack of a strong central government to build the country up from a loose confederation of states. After the war, the country was in the depths of an economic depression due to all the debt held by individuals and the states that financed the war.

Hamilton did play a key role in events leading up to the drafting of the United States Constitution. A national political convention was held in September of 1786 at Mann's Tavern in Annapolis, Maryland, with the purpose of regulating trade between the states. Representing New York State as one of the delegates was Alexander Hamilton. The small convention of only twelve delegates did produce a final report to Congress which called for a broader constitutional convention to be held the following May in Philadelphia.

Hamilton, who was then serving as an assemblyman from New York County in the New York State Legislature, was chosen as a delegate to the Constitutional Convention by his father-in-law, Philip Schuyler. Hamilton was a member of the three-member team and was, of the three, the only one in support of a strong central government.

While at the convention, he served on two committees, one on rules in the beginning of the convention and the other on style at the end of the convention. Hamilton gave a long six-hour speech on June 18 where he presented his own ideas of how a national government should function. His plan allowed the national government nearly unlimited power over the states and called for elected senators and a president that served for a life term. His fellow New York delegate, Robert Yates, described Hamilton's speech as "praised by everybody, but supported by none."

Hamilton's role in drafting the Constitution was minor. He only attended the session from May 27 to June 29 and was absent in July and most of August. In a letter to George Washington, he stated that he felt the convention was a "mere waste of time"; however, he did return to Philadelphia in September to sign the completed Constitution.

By the end of the convention, Hamilton was not completely satisfied with the Constitution, but signed it since it was a vast improvement over the Articles of Confederation. Because the other two New York delegates had already withdrawn, Hamilton was the only delegate from New York to sign the document.

Hamilton's role in the drafting of the Constitution was without distinction; however, he played a much larger role in the ratification process. Even though he had reservations about parts of the Constitution, he felt that this was the best that could be expected under the circumstances and he knew if the document was not ratified by all the states, the results would most likely be "disunion, anarchy, and misery." Along with James Madison and John Jay, Hamilton embarked on a series of essays that became known as *The Federalist Papers*. This series of articles was printed in newspapers all over the country and aggressively defended the new Constitution and explained the implications. Hamilton's first publication supporting the

Constitution appeared in the New York *Independent Journal* in October of 1787. Hamilton, John Jay, and James Madison continued writing articles for the *Independent Journal* and other papers until April 1788. Of the 85 papers constituting *The Federalist Papers*, Hamilton wrote 51 himself. In one essay, Hamilton describes the decision America must make: "Whether societies of men are really capable or not of establishing good government from reflection and choice, or whether they are forever destined to depend for their political constitutions on accident and force." The combined works representing *The Federalist Papers* has become a major classic work in the field of political science and has been published widely and translated into different languages. The current Supreme Court of the United States refers to the papers for guidance on the meaning and interpretation of the Constitution.

Figure – Signing of the Constitution

In addition to Hamilton playing a role on the national scale, promoting the ratification of the Constitution by the states, he was also key in promoting ratification within his own state of New York. At the New York ratification convention held in Poughkeepsie in June 1788, approximately one-third of the delegates were for ratification. Hamilton pored all his energies into winning enough delegates to support ratification. Hamilton's efforts paid off when the New York delegation agreed to ratification of the Constitution by a hair. The vote was close, with 30 for ratification and 27 against. This was a great personal triumph for the young politician.

CHAPTER 4

Secretary of the Treasury

A national debt, if it is not excessive, will be to us a national blessing. – Alexander Hamilton

Shortly after George Washington's inauguration as president in April 1789, Washington nominated Hamilton to become the Secretary of the Treasury and the Senate quickly approved him without debate. His father-in-law, Senator Philip Schuyler, voted for Hamilton's confirmation. Hamilton wrote later of the position, "I conceived myself to be under an obligation to lend my aid towards putting the machine of government in some regular motion."

As one of his accomplishments as Secretary of the Treasury, Hamilton was able to establish firm credit for the young country, which would allow borrowing of money in the future on reasonable terms. Hamilton worked to organize the nation's chaotic finances, gathered information, established standards and procedures, and devised a plan to restore the nearly bankrupt country to financial solvency. At the end of the Revolutionary War, each of the states had acquired large public debts on their balance sheets. Hamilton wanted the central government to assume this debt from the states. The total debt incurred by the individual states and the Confederation government was around 79 million dollars. Of this, two-thirds was national debt; the rest was owed by the states. Hamilton proposed to redeem the debt at par — thereby delivering a windfall to the speculators who had purchased much of the debt instruments at a deep discount. Hamilton reasoned that if the government paid the speculators only what they had paid, their risk of having purchased the debt notes would go unrewarded. In Hamilton's mind, paying the notes at less than par value would effectively be admitting to a partial default on the debt and this would damage the credit of the new government and defeat the purpose of his plan. Hamilton felt it necessary for the United States to pay its debts as quickly as possible to establish faith in the new government. He would later state: "States, like individuals who observe their engagements, are respected and trusted."

Hamilton's credit plan caused division within the Congress and the country. Critics charged the Treasury Secretary with planning to deliver the republic into the hands of speculators. Congressman Benjamin Rush of Pennsylvania rejected Hamilton's credit plan and declared, "It is to nations what private credit and loan offices are to individuals…It begets debt, extravagance, vice, and bankruptcy…I sicken every time I contemplate the European vices that the Secretary's gambling report will necessarily introduce into our infant republic." It was the opposition from James Madison that carried the most weight. Madison had shared Hamilton's belief in a strong national government before and during the Constitutional Convention, but now the Representative from Virginia in the House of Representatives was reconsidering his position. Hamilton knew that without Madison's support, his plan was virtually dead. Hamilton had a strongly held conviction that his plan was sound and sought the help of Thomas Jefferson, Washington's Secretary of State. In the summer of 1790, the rift between Jefferson and Hamilton wasn't fully in bloom and the two were still on working terms.

Figure – Thomas Jefferson, Third President of the United States

Jefferson was not happy with assumption, but as a member of the administration rather than a member of the House, he felt less attached to his fellow Virginians and more concerned about the national good. Jefferson agreed to do what he could do to further Hamilton's debt assumption plan. Soon Jefferson invited Hamilton and Madison to his home for dinner one evening. The pressing issues of the day were the assumption of debt and the location of the nation's capital. The Virginians wanted the capital of the country to be located more centrally rather than in the north-eastern cities of New York and Philadelphia. The bargain struck at the dinner table that evening would give the Northerners assumption and the Southerners the capital. The plan was for the government to meet in Philadelphia for ten years and then move to the banks of the Potomac River. None of the three admitted at the time that a deal had been struck at the dinner table; it wasn't until after decisive votes had been cast that the matter came to light.

In 1791, Hamilton created a central bank for both deposits and borrowing. The First Bank of the United States had an initial capital stock of ten million dollars. The national bank had powerful opponents in Madison, Jefferson, and Attorney General Edmund Randolph, who declared the bank to be an unconstitutional over-extension of the powers of the federal government. President Washington requested that Hamilton defend the proposal, for which he prepared a lengthy report arguing that the Constitution gives Congress "implied powers." Washington agreed with Hamilton's position and signed the bill into law. The bank was very successful, with notes is-sued by the bank trading at face value. Up until 1811, the year the bank's charter expired, The First Bank of the United States served as the fiscal foundation and allowed for rapid expansion of the US economy.

Hamilton's vision for the new country was far-reaching. In his 1791 *Report on Manufactures*, he proposed a tariff designed mainly for the protection of fledgling industrial concerns so that they could prosper with minimal competition from for-eign businesses. Hamilton was wanting to grow the industrial and manufacturing base of the country rather than the agri-cultural sector. His plan faced opposition in Congress and was not adopted.

One of the accomplishments of Hamilton as Secretary of the Treasury was to bring order to the coinage system and establish a mint. Up until that time, the various types of foreign money, trade tokens, and state issued coins, and a variety of currencies, served as mediums of exchange for small and large transac-tions. The array of different types of money made all types of transactions, from the purchase of a bag of flour to large land transactions, cumbersome. Hamilton established the dollar as the unit for the new coinage system which would be based on gold and silver. The mint's capability for production was very limited and it would take decades before significant volumes of coinage were produced, thus allowing systems of commerce to depend solely on the dollar based system.

Figure – Early United States Gold Coin

In order for the government to fund the consolidation of the public debt form the Revolutionary War, new sources of revenue were needed. In 1791, Hamilton promoted an excise tax on distilled spirits, of which whiskey was the dominant product impacted by the new tax, and the new tax went into effect in 1791. The new tax was not well received as the distillers of Western Pennsylvania were on the fringe of the new nation and were not well represented in the Congress. To them, this was nothing more than taxation without representation. The structure of the tax gave an advantage to larger distillers and placed more of a burden on smaller producers. Protests and demonstrations erupted, with tax collectors being harassed and intimidated.

The protests and the lack of tax payments persisted until the events came to a head in 1794. Hamilton and President Washington believed something must be done so they assembled a militia force of thirteen thousand men and marched into Western Pennsylvania. The overwhelming force brought the revolt to an end and the net result was that about 20 men were arrested, all of whom were eventually acquitted or pardoned. The whiskey tax proved difficult to enforce and was eventually repealed in 1801 when Thomas Jefferson and the Republicans came into power.

Figure – Tax Collector Being Tarred and Feathered during the Whiskey Rebellion.

During Hamilton's tenure as Secretary of the Treasury, he implemented many innovative ideas that turned out to be remarkably effective for the country. As with any change, there was opposition to his policies from the Jeffersonian Republicans and others in the government. After his resignation from the Treasury in 1795, he wrote, "I met with many intrinsic difficulties, and many artificial ones proceeding from passions, not very worth, common to human nature, and which act with peculiar force in republics."

CHAPTER 5

The Maria Reynolds Affair

Men are rather reasoning than reasonable animals, for
the most part governed by the impulse of passion.
– Alexander Hamilton

In 1791, Hamilton became embroiled in an affair with a lovely young woman that would cost him dearly — personally, politically, and financially. Living alone in Philadelphia during the summer, while his wife and children were away on vacation, Hamilton was approached by a 23-year-old woman named Maria Reynolds. Maria's story was that she was originally from New York, like Hamilton, and that her scoundrel of a husband had abandoned her and their young daughter and she needed travel money to return to New York to live with family. Hamilton, not having the necessary money on him at the time, agreed to bring the money to her later. As Hamilton would tell of the encounter when he delivered the money, "I took the bill out of my pocket and gave it to her. Some conversation ensued from which it was quickly apparent that nothing other than pecuniary consolation would be acceptable." This was the start of an affair that would last for nearly two years.

During the course of the affair, Maria's husband, James Reynolds, returned to Philadelphia and discovered the affair and decided to profit from the relationship. Hamilton became the target of James Reynolds' blackmail scheme, as Reynolds demanded $1000 for his silence and stated he would take the daughter and leave the area for good. Hamilton paid the money; however, that was not the end of Reynolds' demands for money. Reynolds moved back in with Maria and allowed the affair to continue, occasionally asking Hamilton for small sums of money.

Blackmail was not James Reynolds' only vice; he had been involved in a scheme to defraud Revolutionary War veterans out of their pensions and the law had caught up with him and he was put in jail. Reynolds contacted Hamilton for assistance but he refused to help. Reynolds was enraged by Hamilton's refusal and put word out to Hamilton's rivals in the Republican party of a scandal that would bring down the Federalist hero. James Monroe, Congressmen Frederick Muhlenberg, and Abraham Venable visited Reynolds in jail and were told a tale of the home-wrecking Hamilton, and Reynolds also claimed that his scheme to defraud the veterans was part of Hamilton's doings. Of course, the part about the blackmail payments was omitted from Reynolds' story.

In December 1792, Monroe and Muhlenberg approached Hamilton with Reynolds' story and letters from Maria that she claimed Hamilton had sent her. Hamilton admitted to the affair and told the gentlemen that in no way was there involvement with the Treasury Department. Hamilton gave the men letters from Maria to validate his story. Monroe and Muhlenberg believed his story and felt this was a personal matter and not part of a government scandal. Hamilton was relieved and believed this sordid part of his life was behind him — little did he know that this was not the end of the story.

While Monroe did keep the affair from the public eye, he did make copies of the letters and sent them to Thomas Jefferson. Jefferson was the head of the rival Republican Party and would within a few years use these letters to his advantage to disgrace his rival, Hamilton. Five years later, in 1797, Jefferson used his knowledge of the affair to start rumors about Hamilton's private life. The sordid details of the affair would come into the public eye by a series of pamphlets authored by the muckraking journalist James Callender. Included in the pamphlets were excerpts from the letters Hamilton had given to Monroe years before. Hamilton was outraged and approached Monroe, who denied involvement. The row between the two men turned bitter and Monroe challenged Hamilton to a duel. The duel was averted by the intervention of Aaron Burr, the United States Senator from New York.

Figure – Aaron Burr

Hamilton responded to Callender's pamphlets with his own 95-page pamphlet entitled *Observations on Certain Documents.* In the pamphlet, he denied all charges of corruption, but did not deny his affair with Maria Reynolds; rather, he apologized publicly for his moral failure. Hamilton wrote of the incident: "This confession is not made without a blush. I cannot be the apologist of any vice because the ardor of passion may have made it mine. I can never cease to condemn myself for the pang which it may inflict in a bosom eminently entitled to all my gratitude, fidelity, and love. But that bosom will approve, that, even at so great an expense, I should effectually wipe away a more serious stain from a name which it cherishes with no less elevation than tenderness. The public, too, will, I trust, excuse the confession. The necessity of it to my defence against a more heinous charge could alone have extorted from me so painful an indecorum." The public scandal over the affair severely damaged Hamilton's reputation, not to mention that it caused family strife between himself and Elizabeth.

Before publication of the pamphlet by Hamilton, Maria Reynolds sued her husband for divorce and as an odd coincidence of fate, used Aaron Burr as her attorney.

Not to overshadow all of Alexander Hamilton's brilliant work as statesman and public servant, he does hold the dubious distinction of being involved in America's first public sex scandal by a high ranking government official.

CHAPTER 6

Return to Private Life

The sacred rights of mankind are not to be rummaged for among old parchments or musty records. They are written, as with a sunbeam, in the whole volume of human nature, by the hand of the divinity itself; and can never be erased.
– Alexander Hamilton

After his resignation as Secretary of the Treasury in 1795, he moved the family back to New York City to devote himself to his wife and seven children and resume his law practice. Now a private citizen, Hamilton could not resist the political arena and played some role, for good or ill, in the world of politics. Hamilton assisted his old friend George Washington in preparing his 1796 Farewell Address to the nation.

Hamilton was also drafted by Washington to serve under him again in the Army as the nation was preparing for possible war with France. John Adams, who was the second president, was not supportive of having Hamilton in a leadership role in the Army. Adams feared that Hamilton had imperial plans for the Army and would use it to punish his Republican enemies and conquer new land. In February 1799, Adams announced a new peace mission with France. This shocked the Hamiltonians and they accused Adams of submitting to the French. They even accused Adams of ruining the Federalist Party. There were several reasons behind Adams planning this peace mission. First, Adams wanted to weaken Hamilton's power. Secondly, he realized that support for militarism was fading away as the political enthusiasm among the masses was dying down; the public was annoyed that it had to pay higher taxes to maintain the Army and became critical of the Sedition Act. Thirdly, his preference for peace over war influenced the motive of a peace mission, and he realized that if his peace mission succeeded, he would have fair chances of being re-elected. The second peace mission to France was successful and the tensions between France and America subsided; thus, war was averted and the Army was soon disbanded.

The election of 1796 was the first test of the two political ideologies embodied by the two parties. The Federalists nominated Adams for president and Thomas Pickering as vice president. The Republicans choices were Thomas Jefferson for president and Aaron Burr for vice president. Each member of the Electoral College was allowed to cast two votes for their choice of president. The candidate with the most votes was the victor and the new president. The second place finisher would become the vice president. Adams won the presidential election by a narrow margin of three electoral votes. Hamilton was actively involved in the election, attempting to make Thomas Pickering the president. His efforts failed and had the effect of making Thomas Jefferson the vice president. The Federalist Adams would be the president and his opponent, Thomas

Jefferson from the opposing party, would be vice president. Adams started serving as the president with Jefferson as the antagonistic vice president.

President Adams did not trust Hamilton and didn't seek his help in his administration. From Adams' letters we learn of his thoughts on Hamilton: "Bastard brat of a Scotch peddler, who was as ambitious as Bonaparte, though less courageous, and, save for me, would have involved us in a foreign war with France and a civil war with ourselves."

Figure – John Adams, Second President of the United States

Adams ran for second term as president in the election of 1800 but was in third place behind Jefferson and Burr. There was an electoral college vote tie between Jefferson and Burr which threw the election into the House of Representatives to be decided. Hamilton was in opposition to both men; the choice was between the "demagogic" Jefferson and the "despicable" Burr. Hamilton disliked Jefferson politically, but for Burr his dislike was more personal and deep-seated. In a person letter in 1792, he wrote of Burr: "I feel it to be a religious duty to oppose his career." In the election of 1800, Hamilton used his considerable personal influence with Federalist congressmen to prevent Burr from winning the presidency. Through Hamilton's efforts to thwart Burr's advancement, he reluctantly helped Jefferson win the election, and by default, Burr became the vice president.

Chapter 7

Like Father Like Son – Duels to the Death

When the sword is once drawn, the passions of men observe no bounds of moderation. – Alexander Hamilton

Hamilton's eldest son, Phillip, was nearly twenty years of age in 1801, with good looks, intelligence, and a cordial manner; he was destined to replicate his father's rise to prominence. Hamilton regarded Phillip as the family's „eldest and brightest hope" and was grooming him to great things. Phillip attended a Fourth of July celebration and heard a speech by a young Republican lawyer, George Eacker. His speech was full of partisan rancor and besmirched the reputation of his father. Young Phillip and a friend tracked down Eacker and his party later and harassed them at a theater. The conflict between the men escalated until a duel for honor was thrown down. John Church, Phillip's uncle, tried unsuccessfully to negotiate a truce to avert a duel. Eacker would not back down and a duel was set for 3:00pm the next day across the Hudson River at Paulus Hook, New Jersey. At the duel, Philip followed his father's advice and did not raise his pistol at the command to fire. Eacker's shot hit Philip above the hip with the bullet lodging in his left arm. Phillip got off a shot just before he slumped to the ground. Philip was rushed back across the river to Manhattan for medical care.

Once Alexander Hamilton learned the negotiations had failed, he rushed to the house of the family physician, Dr. David Hosack, to inform him that his professional service might soon be needed. Hosack, already aware of the duel, hurried to the home of John and Angelica Church, where Philip had already been brought. Hosack said of the young man's condition: "He instantly turned from the bed and, taking me by the hand, which he grasped with all the agony of grief, he exclaimed in a tone and manner that can never be effaced from my memory, 'Doctor, I despair.'" Soon Alexander and Elizabeth arrived on the scene. The couple hung to their dying son throughout the long night. After professing his belief in Christ, Philip Hamilton died early in the morning. Phillip's funeral was attended by large crowds of mourners. George Eacker was not prosecuted for Phillip's death; however, he was not long for this world either, as he was to die of consumption in two years.

The death was hard on the family, especially affected was Phillip's younger sister, Angelica. Angelica, being very close to her brother, became unstable and had a nervous breakdown as a result of the stress of her brother's untimely death. Hamilton focused his attention on the troubled daughter in hopes that she would bounce back from the tragedy. She would not recover and would spend the rest of her long life in the care of doctors. She had periods of relative normalcy but would lapse into long periods where she would revert back to her childhood and did not recognize family members. After Phillip's death, Hamilton lapsed into despair. His friend Robert Troup wrote of Hamilton: "Never did I see a man so completely overwhelmed with grief as Hamilton has been."

In June 1804, Vice President Burr learned of Hamilton's disparaging remarks about his character and asked Hamilton for an explanation or a public apology. After additional correspondence between the two, the conversation digressed to the point where Burr issued the challenge of a duel. Hamilton felt he was bound by honor to accept Burr's request for a duel.

Figure – Duel between Hamilton and Burr

The night before the duel, Hamilton wrote a letter to his wife in defense of his planned action and enclosed his last will and testament. In the letter he declared he wished to avoid the duel and he claimed "no ill will to Col. Burr, distinct from political opposition, which as I trust, has proceeded from pure and upright motives." Hamilton had planned on exposing himself to Burr's fire without retaliation: "I have resolved, if our interview is conducted in the usual manner, and it pleases God to give me the opportunity, to reserve and throw away my first fire, and I have thoughts even of reserving my second fire — and thus giving a double opportunity to Col. Burr to pause and reflect." To Hamilton, his intentions were not suicidal, rather a gallant gamble to preserve his honor.

The duel took place in the early morning of July 11, 1804, on the banks of the Hudson River at Weehawken, New Jersey. Hamilton's party in the duel was made up of his physician, Dr. David Hosack, and his loyal associate, Nathaniel Pendleton. Hamilton borrowed a dueling pistol, which could be set with a hair trigger, from his brother-in-law, John Church. This was the same pistol used by Phillip Hamilton in his fatal duel just three years earlier. Burr was assisted by his long time protégé, William Van Ness. Burr and Hamilton were very different men; though similar in size and age, Burr's background and family ancestry was that of a well born aristocrat, while Hamilton's background was that of an illegitimate orphan from a family without distinction or class. Years of conflict between the men had drawn them to this critical point in their lives.

The exact events of the duel are in debate by historians. Some say that Hamilton did not fire his pistol and others say he fired into the air. Without doubt, Burr fired one shot and struck Hamilton in the lower abdomen with a mortal blow.

Hamilton was taken by boat back across the Hudson River to the home of his old friend, William Bayard, Jr., who had been waiting on the dock. By the time Hamilton reached the bed at Bayard's house, he was nearly comatose. Dr. Hosack undressed him and administered a large dose of anodyne, a strong pain killer. During the day, the physician administered an opium and cider potion, called laudanum, for the pain. Hamilton was in a great deal of pain and according to Hosack „his suffering during the whole day was almost intolerable." Though Hamilton was not a particularly religious man, he hadn't gone to church since the Revolution, he did call for a minister to be at his bedside. It was noon of the day after the duel before Elizabeth and their seven children could reach Hamilton's bedside. Elizabeth had not been told the truth of the gravity of the situation and became frantic when she found her husband on his deathbed. On July 12, 1804, in the early afternoon, Alexander Hamilton passed from this world with his sister-in-law, Angelica Schuyler Church, and his bishop at his bedside. At the age of forty-nine, his work was complete but his legacy would live on. Just as quickly as the duel put an end to Hamilton's life, so did it end the political career of Aaron Burr.

The funeral procession in New York City was enormous, with thousands of people paying tribute to this famous American.

Governor Morris gave the eulogy at the funeral and established a fund to support Elizabeth and the children. Alexander Hamilton was laid to rest in the Trinity churchyard cemetery in Manhattan.

Elizabeth Hamilton would outlive Alexander by decades and die at age 97. She would remain an ardent supporter of her husband's legacy until her death.

Chronology

1755 - January 11: Alexander Hamilton born on the British Island of Nevis in the West Indies. Several biographers' accounts put the year of Hamilton's birth as 1757.

1765 - The Hamiltons move to the island of St. Croix. James Hamilton leaves his family and Alexander will never see his father again.

1766 - Alexander begins work at the St Croix counting house owned by Nicholas Cruger.

1768 - February 19: Alexander's mother, Rachel Fawcett, dies of yellow fever. Alexander nearly dies as well.

1773 - Nicholas Cruger and a small group of local people provide funds to send Alexander away to New Jersey for grammar school.

1774 - Hamilton begins study at King's College and writes his first political pamphlet.

1775 - April 19: First shots of the American Revolution are fired at the battles of Lexington and Concord.

1776 - March 14: Hamilton becomes captain of the 1st Battalion, 5th Field Artillery Unit. December 26: Hamilton's artillery unit takes part in Washington's successful capture of

Trenton, New Jersey.

1777 - George Washington promotes Hamilton to lieutenant colonel and makes him aide-de-camp.

1778 - Hamilton fights in the battle of Monmouth, New Jersey.

1780 - December 14: Hamilton marries Elizabeth Schuyler.

1781 - February 16: Hamilton and Washington quarrel following the general's accusation that Hamilton has shown disrespect. October 14: Hamilton leads combined American and French soldiers in a successful charge against a fortified British position at Yorktown, Virginia. November: Hamilton leaves active military service.

1782 - January 22: Elizabeth gives birth to their first child named Phillip. July: Hamilton is made receiver of continental taxes for New York. November: Hamilton arrives in Philadelphia as a representative to the Continental Congress.

1783 – September: The Treaty of Paris officially ends the American Revolution. The Hamiltons take up residence at 57 Wall Street in New York City.

1784 - June 29: Hamilton argues his first Trespass Act case in the Mayor's Court of the City of New York. September: Elizabeth gives birth to a second child named Angelica.

1785 - February 4: Hamilton and 31 others set for the guiding principles for an anti-slavery group, the New York Society for

Promoting the Manumission of Slaves.

1786 – April: Hamilton is elected to the New York legislature. May: Third Hamilton child is born, named Alexander. September: Delegates at the Annapolis Convention issue a report drafted by Hamilton to all 13 states, recommending that a general convention be called to render an American government adequate to meet the needs of the Union.

1787 – May: The Constitutional Convention convenes in Philadelphia and Hamilton is one of three New York delegates. October: Hamilton, James Madison, and John Jay begin writing a series of essays that are known as *The Federalist Papers*.

1788 – April: A fourth child, James, is born to the Hamiltons. July 26: The State of New York becomes the eleventh state to ratify the Constitution.

1789 - George Washington becomes first president of the United States and nominates Hamilton to be the first Secretary of the Treasury.

1790 – January: Hamilton submits his "First Report on the Public Credit" to Congress. June 20: Hamilton dines at the New York home of Secretary of State Thomas Jefferson and strikes a deal with James Madison which will ensure Virginia's support of federal assumption of state debts in exchange for Hamilton's agreement to encourage northern members of Congress to move the nation's capital to a southern site on the banks of the Potomac River. December: Hamilton submits a report to the House calling for the chartering of a national bank.

1791 – Jefferson and Madison form the Republicans, the nation's first opposition political party. In an election for the New York Senate seat, the Republican, Aaron Burr, defeats incumbent Philip Schuyler. This begins the political rivalry between Burr and Hamilton. Hamilton begins an affair with Maria Reynolds.

1792 – Hamilton is accused by the Republicans of financial impropriety and they investigate him. Bitter political wrangling between Hamilton's Federalists and Jefferson's Republicans will dominate the national press and convulse the President's cabinet. August: John Church, the fifth child, is born to the Hamiltons. A mint is established.

1793 – April: Washington issues a proclamation of neutrality toward France. August: A Yellow Fever outbreak begins in Philadelphia, causing most of the residents to flee the city. Both Hamilton and his wife Elizabeth contract the disease but eventually recover. Jefferson resigns as Secretary of State, leaving Hamilton in a commanding position in Washington's cabinet.

1794 – Hamilton assists in the suppression of the "Whiskey Rebellion."

1795 – Hamilton submits his final financial report to Congress and resigns as Treasury Secretary. February: Hamilton and his family leave Philadelphia and return to New York where he returns to his law practice.

1796 - Hamilton assists Washington with his farewell address. John Adams, who has been vice president for two terms, becomes the second President of the United States.

1797 – Schuyler defeats Burr and is re-elected to the US Senate. A pamphlet published by James Callender accuses Hamilton of financial and marital improprieties with Maria Reynolds. August: William Stephen, the sixth child of the Hamiltons, is born.

1798 – Relationships between France and the United States disintegrate due to failure of the American peace mission. President Adams names George Washington as head of the US Army. To Adams' dismay, Washington insists that Hamilton be made inspector general and second in command of the Army.

1799 – November: A seventh child, Eliza, is born to the Hamiltons. December 14: George Washington dies.

1800 – John Adams loses presidency to Thomas Jefferson. Hamilton drops support for Adams and backs Jefferson. Hamilton begins constructing a home in upper Manhattan, naming it "The Grange."

1801 – February 17: The House makes Jefferson President on the thirty-sixth ballot. November 16: Hamilton and a number of other leading Federalists found the *The New York Evening Post*. November 23: Philip Hamilton, in an attempt defend his father's honor, challenges George Eacker to a duel. Phillip is mortally wounded and dies the next day.

1802 – Hamilton and his family move into the Grange. June: The last child, named Philip, is born to the Hamiltons.

1804 – April: A letter is published asserting that Hamilton has expressed a "despicable opinion" of Aaron Burr. A series of letters between Burr and Hamilton are exchanged, resulting in a duel being scheduled for July 11. July 11: Hamilton is mortally wounded by Burr in the duel at Weehawken, New Jersey. Hamilton dies the next day from the gunshot. July 14: A massive funeral is held in New York for Hamilton.

1854 – November 9: Elizabeth Hamilton dies at the age of 97.

Acknowledgments

I would like to thank Lisa Zahn for her help in preparation of this book. Unless otherwise noted, all the photographs are from the public domain.

Further Reading

Chernow, Ron. *Alexander Hamilton*. Penguin Books. 2004.

Conant, Charles A. and Doug West. *Alexander Hamilton – Illustrated and Annotated*. C&D Publications. 2015.

Randall, Willard S. *Alexander Hamilton - A Life*. Perennial. 2003.

About the Author

Doug West is a retired engineer, small business owner, and experienced non-fiction writer with several books to his credit. His writing interests are general, with expertise in science, history, biographies, numismatics, and "How To" topics. Doug has a B.S. in Physics from the Missouri School of Science and Technology and a Ph.D. in General Engineering from Oklahoma State University. He lives with his wife and little dog, "Scrappy," near Kansas City, Missouri. Additional books by Doug West can be found at http://www.amazon.com/Doug-West/e/B00961PJ8M. Follow the author on Facebook at: https://www.facebook.com/30minutebooks.

Figure – Doug West (photo by Karina Cinnante)

Additional Books by Doug West

A Short Biography of the Scientist Sir Isaac Newton

A Short Biography of the Astronomer Edwin Hubble

Galileo Galilei – A Short Biography

Benjamin Franklin – A Short Biography

The American Revolutionary War – A Short History

Coinage of the United States – A Short History

John Adams – A Short Biography

In the Footsteps of Columbus (Annotated) Introduction and Biography Included (with Annie J. Cannon)

Alexander Hamilton – Illustrated and Annotated (with Charles A. Conant)

Harlow Shapley – Biography of an Astronomer

How to Write, Publish and Market Your Own Audio Book

Index

Made in the USA
Middletown, DE
25 August 2022

72162329R00036